Original title:
Unseen Scars

Copyright © 2024 Swan Charm
All rights reserved.

Author: Kaido Väinamäe
ISBN HARDBACK: 978-9916-79-069-4
ISBN PAPERBACK: 978-9916-79-070-0
ISBN EBOOK: 978-9916-79-071-7

The Quiet Chronicles

In the stillness of the night,
Stars blink softly, a gentle light.
Memories linger, like fading dreams,
Time whispers secrets, or so it seems.

A lone leaf dances on the breeze,
Carried by whispers, meant to please.
The world hushed beneath a silver glow,
As the quiet tales begin to flow.

Footsteps tread on the worn-out path,
Each moment marked, a subtlemath.
Stories woven in the fabric of time,
In every silence, a hidden rhyme.

Beneath the surface, where shadows play,
Lives a truth that won't fade away.
Unseen glances, in the rearview,
The heart knows love, old yet new.

At dawn's first touch, the quiet breaks,
A symphony rises, the silence aches.
In every breath, the chronicles lie,
Waiting to spark, to soar, to fly.

Whispers in the Shadows

In corners dark where secrets sleep,
Whispers echo, quiet and deep.
Silent stories that time forgot,
In the heart of shadows, a hidden plot.

Moonlight spills on the cobblestone,
A dance of dreams, where spirits roam.
Each flicker of light holds an unseen tale,
Of love, of loss, in the midnight veil.

Echoes of laughter, soft like sighs,
Drift through the night beneath vast skies.
A tapestry woven of dusk and dawn,
In whispered shades, we're reborn.

Footprints lingering where few have tread,
In silent places, the brave have fled.
Yet every shadow, a voice so clear,
In whispers' embrace, we draw near.

The night holds magic, if you dare seek,
In whispered riddles, the shadows speak.
Unravel the secrets, with careful grace,
For in the dark lies a sacred space.

Marks of a Silent Struggle

Beneath the weight of hidden scars,
Silent battles marked with stars.
Each whisper lingers in the night,
Fading echoes, out of sight.

In rooms where shadows softly blend,
Dreams retreat, and hopes suspend.
Eyes like lanterns, dimmed and tired,
Yet within them, a heart's fire.

Words unspoken, heavy air,
Secrets carried, burdens shared.
Silent warriors, weary yet bold,
Their stories silenced, truths untold.

A faint spark in the cold embrace,
Witness to the hidden race.
In the calm, beneath the strife,
We find the essence of our life.

Marks of bravery, etched in skin,
Each moment lost, a quiet win.
In the struggle, we uncover gold,
Resilience shines, a force untold.

Ghosts in the Fabric of Life

Threads of memory weave and spin,
Echoes floating, where we've been.
Ghosts of laughter, shadows of tears,
Stitching together our deepest fears.

In the quiet, they softly call,
Whispers linger, memories crawl.
Through the fabric, they intertwine,
In every stitch, a forgotten line.

Patches worn from time and wear,
Stories tangled, textured air.
Each ghost a song, a silent plea,
Nestled deep in the seams of me.

In sunlight's glow, they dance and play,
Reviving moments lost in gray.
Every thread holds a spirit's breath,
Through life's loom, they tease at death.

In the fabric, we find our place,
A mélange of time, a sacred space.
Ghosts of joy and sorrow blend,
In the weave, our stories send.

Unspoken Fables of the Soul

In shadows deep, the stories hide,
Tales of longing, truth belied.
Each fable breathes in silence still,
A yearning heart, a quiet will.

Through twilight dreams, they start to weave,
Threads of hope that we believe.
In every glance, an ancient tale,
Of love unfound and hearts set sail.

Unspoken words, a tender sigh,
Secrets nestled where wishes lie.
The soul sings soft, its language pure,
In whispered verses, we endure.

Countless fables, lost in time,
Echoes soft as a lullaby rhyme.
Each tale a journey, a sacred art,
Painting the canvas of the heart.

In silence, wisdom finds a way,
To tell the stories that won't stay.
Unspoken fables, softly spun,
Illuminate the path we run.

Ink Beneath the Skin

In every mark, a story flows,
Ink beneath skin, where silence grows.
Tales of heartache, joy, and strife,
Written softly, carving life.

The needle's dance, a sacred art,
An imprint deep within the heart.
Each color speaks a truth untamed,
A visual song, forever claimed.

From midnight black to crimson red,
Every shade a word unsaid.
Etched in flesh, like whispered dreams,
A tapestry of hopes and schemes.

Through every line, the journey shows,
Emotions tangled, ebb and flows.
Ink beneath the skin persists,
A canvas of existence kissed.

In moments fleeting, we reflect,
The beauty found in every defect.
Ink beneath skin, a life portrayed,
In every stroke, our souls displayed.

Moonlight on Scarred Ground

Under the silver glow of night,
Peace dances on the damaged earth.
Whispers of the past take flight,
Healing begins with each soft mirth.

Rivers of time flow silently,
Embracing the wounds that still remain.
Roots stretch deep, eternally,
Yearning for solace from the pain.

Stars gather in a watchful trance,
As shadows fade into the dawn.
Nature beckons with a chance,
To rise anew, from what was gone.

Moonlit paths reveal the scars,
Crafted by stories yet untold.
Each shimmer a guide to distant stars,
In darkness, there lies hope untold.

Beneath Layers of Light

In the dawn's gentle embrace,
Secrets hide in the glimmering dew.
Life's tapestry weaves its grace,
Painting dreams in every hue.

Above the noise, stillness reigns,
Whispers of truth softly unfold.
Each moment counted, no more chains,
Courage found in stories bold.

Beneath the surface, magic thrums,
Echoes of history, rich and grand.
Time reveals what beauty becomes,
In the sculpture of the land.

Embers of light begin to dance,
Guiding footsteps through the mist.
Every heartbeat a second chance,
In the warmth of a sunbeam kissed.

Echoes of Resilience

Through the storm, voices emerge,
Carrying tales of silent strength.
Hope rises with each surging surge,
Binding the past with love's length.

Mountains tall, yet hearts stand taller,
Holding steadfast against the fray.
With every fall, we only gather,
The courage to forge a new way.

Roots entwined in the soil's hold,
Nurtured by trials we have faced.
Stories of old in whispers told,
Echo through time, never erased.

In the shadows, light finds a way,
Through cracks in the hurt and the fear.
Resilience blooms like dawn's first ray,
A promise shone bright and clear.

Secrets Under the Surface

In the calm where waters lie,
Mysteries murmur soft and low.
Beneath stillness, questions fly,
Searching for truth in the flow.

Years of silence give way to sound,
As currents churn with tales untold.
In the depths, history is found,
Glimmers of secrets, brave and bold.

Every ripple a page turned,
Chronicles written in ancient waves.
Lessons linger, wisdom earned,
In the shadows where the heart saves.

Dive deep into the serene space,
Where echoes of longing resonate.
Under the surface, find your place,
In heartbeats, the unknown awaits.

Subtle Signs of Survival

In whispers of the dawn, we rise,
With shadows creeping, soft goodbyes.
Each breath a testament, we stand,
A fragile hope held in our hands.

The scars we hide, they tell our tales,
Through storms and trials, love prevails.
In secret glances, strength is found,
In silent battles, we are unbound.

The earth beneath, it bears our weight,
With roots entwined, we navigate.
Through thorns we walk, yet flowers bloom,
In darkest nights, we find our room.

A gentle touch, a knowing smile,
Connections forged through every mile.
Among the ruins, life will thrive,
These subtle signs show we survive.

We rise again with morning light,
Embracing all that feels so right.
Together in this vast expanse,
Our spirits dance, we take the chance.

Behind Closed Doors

In silence, secrets find their home,
Behind the doors where shadows roam.
Whispers linger, stories weave,
A tapestry we dare believe.

The laughter fades to muffled sighs,
As truth hides behind painted lies.
In every glance, the world can see,
The quiet pain that sets us free.

Beneath the surface, hearts collide,
Where hopes are stirred and fears reside.
With heavy hearts, we tread the floor,
Each step a question, wanting more.

The echoes pass through time and space,
Creating comfort, holding grace.
In hidden corners, dreams ignite,
Behind closed doors, we find our light.

A fragile bond, a whispered trust,
In shadows deep, we turn to dust.
Yet in the silence, strength adorns,
The heart beats on, though hope seems worn.

The Language of Invisible Hurt

Unspoken words, they pierce the air,
A subtle glance, a weight we share.
In silence bred, the echoes grow,
The language deep, we seldom show.

Beneath the smiles, the armor worn,
Invisible wounds, we are reborn.
Each heartbeat thuds, a muted call,
In hidden battles, we find our fall.

The eyes betray what lips conceal,
Expressions raw, emotions feel.
In every sigh, a story's spun,
The hurt remains, yet hope's not done.

We seek connection in the pain,
Through whispered dreams, a heart's refrain.
In quiet strength, we rise anew,
The language speaks, it welcomes you.

With tender love, we break the chains,
In every struggle, beauty reigns.
The language of the heart, it grieves,
But in that hurt, the spirit believes.

Silted Memories

In fragments lost, the past we sift,
Silted memories, a mournful gift.
Through layers thick, the glimmers show,
A time once bright, now lost below.

With every touch, the echoes fade,
In dusty corners, dreams are laid.
The whispers linger, faint yet clear,
Ghosts of laughter that we hold dear.

Through tides of time, we navigate,
The paths we walked, the twists of fate.
In sunlit hours, shadows dance,
Silted memories, a fleeting chance.

From faded photographs we glean,
The story woven, once so keen.
In twilight's glow, we hold the made,
The threads of love that never fade.

Though silt may cloud the rivers bend,
The heart remembers, it will send
A gentle pulse back to the light,
Where silted memories take their flight.

Unwrapped Banshees of the Heart

Whispers echo in the night,
Banshees dance in soft moonlight.
Veils of sorrow, thinly worn,
Unravel tales of love forlorn.

Crimson shrouds and shadows play,
In the silence, ghosts still sway.
Heartbeats thrumming like a drum,
Through the stillness, they succumb.

Tales of passion intertwine,
Hearts engaged in twisted line.
Broken pieces softly sigh,
Fragmented dreams that dare to fly.

Fleeting glances, lost in time,
Unwrapped sorrows, cryptic rhyme.
Faded echoes call me home,
In the night, forever roam.

Heartstrings tugged with every beat,
In this dance, we feel complete.
Banshees whisper, love portrayed,
In the silence, life displayed.

The Patchwork of Pain

Stitch by stitch, they gather round,
Threads of sorrow tightly wound.
Life's mosaic, jagged seams,
Painful truths sewn into dreams.

Faded colors, rich and bright,
Each patch tells of endless night.
Frayed edges whisper tales untold,
Worn by time, yet still bold.

Tear-stained fabric, crusted scars,
Hope ignites like distant stars.
Carefully crafted, hearts entwined,
In the chaos, peace we find.

Pieces scattered, yearning hearts,
Finding solace in the arts.
Through the anguish, love reveals,
A tapestry of how it feels.

In the fractures, light will break,
From this patchwork, we awake.
Hearts in tandem, beating strong,
Together in the dance of song.

Loomed in Silence

Threads of silence weave the night,
In the dark, we seek the light.
Every whisper, soft and low,
Lives within the hearts we know.

Gentle rhythms hush the fight,
Binding souls in velvet flight.
Hands of time, they slowly draft,
In this stillness, we are grafted.

Shadows linger, dreams arise,
In the quiet, love defies.
Silken strands of hope we spin,
Together, we let life begin.

In this loom, the fabric glows,
Every heartbeat softly flows.
Woven tightly, fears release,
In the quiet, find our peace.

Loomed in silence, hearts entwined,
In this moment, love aligned.
Every thread a story shared,
In this tapestry, we dared.

The Chisel of Time

Carved like stone, the moments pass,
Time works deftly, like a glass.
Each tick tock, a subtle chime,
Sculpting lives with the chisel of time.

Faces change, yet still remain,
Memories inked with joy and pain.
In the echoes of our minds,
The past and future intertwine.

Chiseled edges, sharp and clear,
Every heartbeat, drawing near.
Crafted by the hands of fate,
In the silence, we articulate.

Fragments lost, yet hope survives,
In each tear, our spirit thrives.
Time's embrace, a gentle guide,
In its arms, we must abide.

With every moment, we endure,
The chisel of time, strong and pure.
In our hearts, stories thrive,
Through the passage, we arrive.

The Depth of Unseen Depths

In shadows where whispers lie,
Secrets sink, never to fly.
Beneath the calm, a storm can brew,
Depths untouched, yet known to few.

Each wave holds a silent plea,
A tale of tides, a mystery.
What treasures dwell beneath the foam,
In hidden realms we call our home.

The silence speaks in subtle ways,
Of hopes and dreams lost in the haze.
The ocean's heart beats slow and deep,
Where dreams are sown, and sorrows creep.

A journey starts where eyes can't see,
The depths of truth, a plea to be.
In every ripple, fear and grace,
We find our fears, we find our place.

With every dive, we learn to feel,
The warmth of love, the chill of steel.
For loss and light entwined in dance,
In unseen depths, we take our chance.

Consequences of Hidden Dreams

In the quiet, dreams reside,
Whispers soft, that we can't hide.
Buried deep in the silent night,
They shape our fate, out of our sight.

Each wish unspoken, a silent weight,
Crafting futures we contemplate.
The spark of hope can light the dark,
In dreams concealed, we leave our mark.

Yet shadows linger, doubts emerge,
As hidden dreams begin to surge.
A flicker of fear can dim the glow,
Blocking paths we long to know.

To face the truth, we must take flight,
Embrace the spark, confront the night.
For every dream that lies asleep,
Holds power strong, too vast to keep.

In the end, we rise or fall,
To dance with visions or lose it all.
Consequences woven tight and deep,
In every promise we choose to keep.

The Burden of Unshared Stories

Words unspoken weigh like stone,
In silent hearts, we stand alone.
Each tale withheld, a heavy cost,
In shadows cast, connection lost.

The laughter shared, the tears unseen,
In every thought, a fragile sheen.
What lives within that never escapes,
Is life confined within its drapes?

We carry burdens, unseen weight,
In every heartbeat, we contemplate.
For stories told can heal the soul,
In shared embrace, we become whole.

Yet fear can shackle, tie the tongue,
The strongest hymns left unsung.
What power lies in words absorbed,
When silence reigns, and hearts are starved?

So let us forge a brighter path,
To share the joy, to face the wrath.
For journeys shared can light the way,
In unshared stories, hope can stay.

Uncharted Waters of Emotion

In stillness lies the heart's own sea,
A tempest fierce, uncharted spree.
Rivers flow where feelings churn,
In depths unknown, we laugh and yearn.

Like sailors lost, we seek the shore,
Waves crash hard, we long for more.
In every swell, a tale unfolds,
Of love and loss, of dreams retold.

The compass spins, as stars align,
In waters deep, our fates entwine.
Emotions rise like tides at night,
Guided by the moon's soft light.

We may drift far, we may stray wide,
But in our hearts, the truth won't hide.
In uncharted waters, we find release,
In every wave, a chance for peace.

So fear not the storms that may appear,
For there lies strength in every tear.
In journey's quest, we learn to swim,
In uncharted realms, our souls grow dim.

The Silent Symphony

In quiet halls, the whispers flow,
Gentle notes of joy and woe.
The heartbeats sync, an unseen band,
Where dreams and hope together stand.

A melody of tender grace,
Each silence holds a hidden space.
The songs we hum under our breath,
A tribute to love, a dance with death.

In shadows where the soft light plays,
The symphony of life conveys.
In every pause, a secret sound,
With every breath, our bonds are found.

We weave the threads from dusk to dawn,
An orchestra of souls reborn.
Each note a journey, each rest a dream,
In silent symphony, we gleam.

Together we create a song,
A harmony where we belong.
Through silent chords, our spirits soar,
In every silence, we want more.

Burdens Worn but Unseen

Beneath the smiles, the shadows lie,
Heavy hearts that strain to fly.
A mountain built of silent grief,
The hidden weight, a shared belief.

Each step we take, a tale untold,
In stoic strength, our souls unfold.
We wear our masks with artful grace,
Concealing struggles we must face.

Yet in the eyes, reflections shine,
A knowing spark, a whispered line.
Though burdens heavy may constrain,
Together, we can bear the strain.

For in this life of trials faced,
Each shared burden is embraced.
With hands united, we will stand,
A tapestry, a stronger band.

So when the night feels cold and long,
Remember, here, you still belong.
These burdens worn, though hard to see,
Connect us all, you and me.

Eclipsed Echoes

Beneath the veil, the silence speaks,
In shadows deep, our spirit seeks.
Echoes lost in twilight's grasp,
The dreams we chase, the truths we clasp.

A haunting call from realms unknown,
Each whisper dances, seeds are sown.
In every dusk, a light concealed,
The depths of night, our fate revealed.

Yet hope persists, a guiding star,
In darkest hours, we've come so far.
With every breath, the echoes flare,
Revealing paths beyond despair.

We weave our tales through shadows cast,
In timeless moments, futures vast.
Eclipsed but not entirely lost,
We gather strength, embrace the cost.

For every echo holds a key,
Each heartbeat sings of unity.
Together in the silent glow,
We find the light where shadows flow.

The Unseen Weight We Carry

In every glance, a story lies,
A weight unseen, beneath the skies.
We walk the paths with heavy hearts,
Each burden borne, a work of art.

Through laughter bright, the pain concealed,
In moments shared, our truths revealed.
A silent cry, a gentle plea,
The weight is shared, you walk with me.

In shadows cast and dreams deferred,
Our spirits sing without a word.
Though trials loom, we still advance,
Together bound in this strange dance.

For every tear that graces skin,
A testament to strength within.
Our burdens worn, yet hope still glows,
In every heart, a story flows.

So side by side, we face the storm,
With unseen weights, we still transform.
Through trials faced, we're never far,
In love's embrace, we find our star.

Journal of Hidden Afflictions

In the pages lined with silence,
Whispers of anguish hide,
Each word a heavy burden,
Trapped within, denied.

Ink bleeds through cracked walls,
Reflecting battles fought,
Memories haunt the margins,
Lessons sought, but naught.

Beneath the surface restless,
A storm brews deep within,
Torn between pain and solace,
Courage veils the sin.

Footnotes of the heartache,
Tell tales of love and loss,
Every tear a testament,
To the weight of the cross.

So I pen this chronicle,
Of shadows long and dark,
Holding tight the secrets,
Leaving always a mark.

Deep Waters of Emotion

Dive beneath the surface,
Where currents twist and shift,
In depths where few discover,
Life's overwhelming gift.

Waves crash with unyielding force,
Pulling at the soul,
Each swell reflects a heartbeat,
Seeking to be whole.

Submerged in liquid twilight,
Lost amidst the haze,
Finding solace in shadows,
In this silent maze.

Rippling like the surface,
Thoughts float to the top,
Each bubble bursting brightly,
Before they pop.

In waters deep and mystic,
Stillness meets the tide,
Where my heart finds freedom,
And the truth can't hide.

The Story Beneath the Smile

A curve of bright facade,
Hides a tale untold,
Behind each cheerful glimmer,
Lives a heart that's cold.

Laughter that seems endless,
Masks the cries unheard,
Joy, a painted armor,
A shield, not a word.

With every painted gesture,
A story lingers near,
But shadows pull the corners,
Of the grin that's sheer.

Underneath the surface,
Lies a heavy weight,
Each smile constructs a fortress,
To guard against fate.

When the laughter quiets down,
And the lights start to fade,
The truth begins to whisper,
In colors once portrayed.

Layers of Untold Truth

Beneath the skin, a canvas,
Painted hues of fear,
In layers made of secrets,
And whispers drawn so near.

Each layer tells a story,
Written with faint ink,
Tracing paths of shadows,
In the eyes' soft blink.

Peeling back the surfaces,
Reveals a fragile core,
Tender tales of heartache,
Etched in pain and more.

Through cracks of understanding,
Light seeps in like a dream,
In each fold of silence,
Truth flows like a stream.

So I gather all the textures,
In a quilt stitched with care,
For beneath life's rich layers,
Beauty often lays bare.

Whispers Beneath the Surface

The river flows with secrets untold,
Beneath the ripples, stories unfold.
In shadows dance the dreams we chase,
Whispers linger in a silent space.

Beneath the moonlight, fears arise,
Reflections dim in midnight skies.
Through gentle winds, we hear their call,
Echoes of love that rise and fall.

A melody of hopes and dreams,
In darkened waters, soft light gleams.
The truth we seek is just a sigh,
In every heart, it will not die.

With every wave, a wish is tossed,
Finding solace in what is lost.
The quiet ripples softly sway,
Holding the past in the light of day.

In deep reflections, we will find,
The whispers of the heart and mind.
Together bound under the stars,
We'll unlock the world's hidden bars.

Shadows of Forgotten Pain

In corners dark, where silence clings,
Shadows of past hold fragile strings.
Faded echoes whisper so low,
Stories of hurt that no one knows.

Each tear a river, each sigh a scar,
Carved in the soul like a distant star.
Yet through the haze of weary night,
Hope flickers softly, dimming the fright.

As branches creak under weight of dreams,
The heart can heal from broken seams.
In every twilight, find your grace,
Embrace the pain, and let it chase.

With every dawn, a chance to mend,
The ties that bind, the broken bend.
In shadows cast, we choose the light,
And from the dark, emerge in flight.

So let the past not hold you tight,
For in the shadows, find your might.
Rise from the ashes, fierce and free,
Transform the pain to victory.

Echoes in the Silence

In quiet moments, echoes swell,
A symphony we know too well.
The hush of night speaks loud and clear,
Whispers of love, whispers of fear.

Beneath the stars, we tread with care,
In solitude, we find what's rare.
Invisible threads pull hearts so tight,
Connecting souls like day and night.

Through veils of time, memories bloom,
In every corner, shadows loom.
Yet in that space, the heart will sing,
To silence, joy and sorrow cling.

With every heartbeat, stories weave,
Tales of what we dare believe.
In the stillness, treasures hide,
Echoes that dare to turn the tide.

So listen closely to the sound,
In silence, magic can be found.
For in the depth, we find our way,
Echoes of life, come what may.

Beneath the Veil of Smiles

Behind each smile a story hides,
A world of joys, a sea of tides.
Beneath the laughter, shadows creep,
In silent depths, the heart will weep.

For every grin, a tear has flowed,
In fragile hearts, deep truths are sowed.
Yet hope remains, a gentle hue,
In every soul, the spark shines through.

Among the smiles, the pain resides,
But kindness blooms where love abides.
Through whispered fears, we rise above,
Each hidden wound nourished by love.

Beneath the surface, dreams ignite,
In fractured tales, we find our light.
The mask we wear, a shield of grace,
That hides the truth in its embrace.

So when you see a smiling face,
Remember well, it's not a race.
For hidden deep in every heart,
Lies beauty that's a work of art.

The Weight of Unheard Cries

In the silence, whispers dwell,
Echoes of stories no one can tell.
Hearts heavy with burdens old,
Dreams wrapped in threads of gold.

Courage hides behind closed doors,
Fighting battles on distant shores.
With every tear, a tale unwinds,
A world of hope, the soul still binds.

Beneath the weight, strength may rise,
From ashes deep, it learns to fly.
Each cry unheard, a song so sweet,
In shadows' depths, our truths repeat.

Echoes in the Shadows

In twilight's grasp, soft voices call,
Each echo dances, shadows fall.
Secrets murmur through the night,
Whispers weaving tales of light.

Footprints linger on the ground,
In quiet spaces, dreams are found.
Memories flutter, hearts unite,
In the silence, we take flight.

Every heartbeat is a song,
In darkness, we feel we belong.
In the stillness, courage glows,
Through shadowed paths, our spirit flows.

A Symphony of Unseen Heartbreak

Between the notes lies a quiet ache,
A symphony born from the heart's break.
Every chord, a hidden tear,
In melodies whispers, love draws near.

Broken strings and silence bare,
Echoes linger in the air.
With every note, a story weaves,
In heart's own pain, the spirit believes.

In unseen realms, our hearts collide,
In sorrow's depth, we still confide.
Pain and beauty, hand in hand,
Creating dreams from grains of sand.

The Quiet Resilience of the Soul

In stillness lies a warrior's might,
Facing storms, embracing light.
With gentle grace, we rise anew,
In shadows' grasp, the truth shines through.

Every setback, a lesson learned,
In silent battles, courage burned.
With steadfast heart, we forge our way,
Through darkest nights, we find our day.

In whispered strength, we learn to stand,
Embracing storms, hand in hand.
The soul's quiet roar pierces the night,
In resilience, we find our light.

Shattered Reflections

In shards of glass, the truth lies bare,
Fragments of dreams, floating in air.
Echoes of laughter, whispers of pain,
In every fracture, memories remain.

A dance of shadows, light slips away,
The heart seeks solace, in night and day.
Pieces of me, scattered like stars,
I gather the light, despite the scars.

Through storms of doubt, I learn to see,
The beauty of chaos, in all of me.
Each splintered thought, a lesson to glean,
In brokenness, I find what's unseen.

Reflections may shift, but I am still strong,
In every discord, I learn the song.
Through shattered fragments, I carve my way,
Embracing the night, welcoming day.

With every piece, I build up again,
From ruins of hope, new beginnings wane.
In shattered reflections, I shape my fate,
Resilience blooms, though I bend, not break.

Mapping the Invisible

In the silence, whispers confide,
Secrets untold, where dreams hide.
Mapping the paths that few have walked,
In shadows of doubt, softly we talked.

Stars in the sky, our guide from afar,
They shine through the night, like wishes to mar.
The compass of heart, leads me through haze,
In the veil of the unknown, I find my ways.

Every heartbeat, a step taken bold,
Navigating whispers, stories unfold.
With eyes wide open, I search for the signs,
In the fabric of fate, the truth intertwines.

Through tangled thoughts, I sketch the unseen,
Drawn to the places where light has been.
Each line I trace, a journey anew,
In mapping the invisible, I forge my view.

With every step, the path becomes clear,
Guided by courage, I shed my fear.
In the depths, I find treasure untold,
As I map the invisible, my spirit unfolds.

The Subtle Art of Endurance

In quiet moments, strength is found,
A gentle pulse, a steadfast sound.
Embracing the weight, I learn to bear,
In the art of endurance, I find my prayer.

Tides may rise and storms may roar,
Yet deep within, I long for more.
Each struggle a brush, painting my soul,
Through the tempest, I become whole.

With patience as armor, I stand my ground,
In the stillness, resilience is crowned.
Unseen battles, fought day by day,
In the subtle art, I find my way.

Navigating shadows, I gather my might,
Through the darkest hour, I seek the light.
A tapestry woven with threads of grace,
In the art of endurance, I find my place.

With every heartbeat, a story unfolds,
In the dance of life, my spirit beholds.
Through trials faced, my heart learns to soar,
Embracing the journey, forevermore.

Threads of Resilience

In the weave of time, strong threads align,
Woven with care, each strand a sign.
Through the tapestry, stories are spun,
In threads of resilience, I find the sun.

Life may fray at the edges we know,
Yet through every challenge, our spirits grow.
Each knot a reminder of battles we face,
In the fabric of courage, I find my place.

With colors bold, my heart takes flight,
In the loom of dreams, I chase the light.
Each tug of the thread, a lesson to learn,
In resilience forged, hope begins to burn.

Through trials and tears, I gather my grace,
Stitching together each fractured space.
In the patterns we weave, strength intertwines,
With threads of resilience, our spirit shines.

As the fabric unfolds, I see the design,
A masterpiece crafted, uniquely mine.
In every strand, a story revived,
With threads of resilience, I feel alive.

Silent Echoes of Pain

In the dark where shadows creep,
Silent echoes of sorrow seep.
Sighs linger in the dampened air,
Yearning hearts heavy with despair.

Beneath the weight of dreams unspun,
Fragments lost, battles not won.
Memories in silence wane and fade,
While hopes dissolve in the plans we laid.

With each heartbeat, a story told,
Of brave souls weary, growing old.
Yet in the silence, a spark may glow,
Set aflame what we dared not show.

Through hidden cracks and creaking doors,
Echoes resound of once-open shores.
Reflections flicker in dimming light,
A call for strength to reclaim the fight.

In the quiet, where shadows loom,
Resilience blooms amidst the gloom.
Finding solace in the chains that bind,
We learn that peace is intertwined.

Shadows Beneath the Surface

Whispers float on a turbulent tide,
Shadows lurking where fears reside.
Beneath the calm, a storm is brewing,
Deep currents hide what is worth pursuing.

Each wave that crashes against the shore,
Carries secrets we cannot ignore.
Rippling depths conceal the pain,
In silence, echoes continue to reign.

With glimmers of truth, we hold our breath,
In the dance of life and the shadow of death.
The surface glistens, a deceptive sight,
While lurking demons wait for the night.

Fingers trace the lines of sorrow,
Searching for light in a dark tomorrow.
Yet in the shadows, a strength does rise,
Emerging fierce beneath clouded skies.

When tides recede, revealing the scars,
We'll chart the course beneath the stars.
Though shadows haunt, we find our way,
Guided by whispers, come what may.

Whispers of Hidden Wounds

Between the laughter and the smiles,
Lie whispers echoing through the miles.
Hidden wounds that bleed in silence,
Speak of loss, of hearts' defiance.

Each scar a story etched in time,
A soft reminder of pain sublime.
Like ink on pages, they mark our trails,
In the depth of night, when courage fails.

Yet through the cracks, we seek the light,
Finding strength in our darkest plight.
These whispers guide us to our peace,
A gentle call for sweet release.

In the absence of words, we belong,
Knowing struggles only make us strong.
Healing comes with every breath,
Turning the shadows into a quest.

So let the whispers softly swell,
In every heart where secrets dwell.
For every wound will one day mend,
A journey of healing that has no end.

The Weight of What's Concealed

In the corners where shadows lay,
The weight of secrets turns to gray.
Beneath the silence, burdens swell,
Each unsaid word, a hidden spell.

Heavy hearts carry tales untold,
Of dreams that shattered, of hopes turned cold.
Yet still we walk with laughter bright,
Wearing masks beneath the light.

With every smile, a piece we hide,
The depth of pain we cannot abide.
But in the dark, the truth will rise,
Breaking free from the heavy lies.

Letting go of what chained our soul,
We seek the riddles to make us whole.
For in the journey, we find a way,
To lighten the load and seize the day.

Together we'll share what once felt wrong,
Finding strength in a united song.
For the weight of what's concealed will fade,
And in our truth, a new path is laid.

Invisible Threads of Loss

In silence, we weave our sighs,
Threads of memory uncurl and rise.
Each moment lingers, a fragile kiss,
A tapestry formed from shadows of bliss.

Lost voices whisper through the night,
In echoes soft as fading light.
We trace the patterns, worn and frayed,
In the fabric of love that time betrayed.

Fingers grasp at what has gone,
Holding on to just a song.
The heartstrings pull, the tears will flow,
As we learn to let the feelings go.

Memories linger like a ghost,
In corners where we love the most.
With every thread, a part of us stays,
Woven tightly through our days.

Yet from the seams, we find the light,
In the darkest moments, hopes take flight.
Invisible threads, we'll never sever,
Bind us together, now and forever.

Ghosts of Yesterday

In the corners of our minds, they dwell,
Whispers of stories too hard to tell.
Footsteps echo in the dampened halls,
As time unveils its haunting calls.

With every twilight, they softly tread,
Flickering shadows of those now dead.
Memories linger with a bittersweet taste,
In their presence, we often feel misplaced.

Old photographs fade, but not the pain,
In the silent rooms where dreams remain.
Faces smile in frames now cracked,
Yet the warmth of love feels overpacked.

Conversations lost in the gentle breeze,
Catch our hearts in moments that freeze.
We carry their voices like gentle rain,
Each drop a reminder of our shared pain.

But amidst the sorrow, we find a path,
A way to honor love's aftermath.
We learn to dance with our ghosts so bright,
Together we stride into the night.

The Unspoken Burden

We carry weights we cannot share,
Invisible loads, heavy and bare.
In silence, we walk our lonely roads,
Beneath the smiles, the silence explodes.

Words unuttered, they drift like dust,
A lingering ache that stirs mistrust.
Our hearts are bruised but still we fight,
Searching for solace in the endless night.

In crowded rooms, we stand apart,
An ocean of hurt fills every heart.
Each laugh a mask, each glance a shield,
To hide the wounds we refuse to yield.

But when the world fades into sleep,
We hold the burdens we can't keep.
With every tear that softly falls,
We find our strength within these walls.

Yet in these shadows, we find the grace,
To share the burden, to face our space.
For in the sake of knowing we are whole,
We unmask the pain and begin to console.

Masks That Never Fit

We wear our masks with practiced ease,
Hiding truths that bring us to our knees.
A smile painted, a laugh rehearsed,
Yet inside, we feel the bubble burst.

In crowded spaces, we play our parts,
But the heaviness weighs on our hearts.
Each layer thickens with every lie,
Underneath, we just want to cry.

Shadows flicker behind closed eyes,
Yearning for freedom from all the ties.
In fragile moments, the truth breaks through,
Reminding us that we are still true.

Yet the masks shield us from the pain,
And we continue the daily strain.
But in the quiet, the whispers call,
To strip away the veil, once and for all.

So in the chaos, we now create,
A place to love, a space to relate.
With every mask that we shed in trust,
We reveal the beauty of being just.

The Unseen Path of Resilience

In shadows deep, we find our strength,
A journey long, yet full of grace.
Each step we take, with heart and length,
We rise again, we find our place.

Through storms that rage, and winds that howl,
A whisper calls from deep within.
With every tear, we learn to grow,
And smile again, it's where we begin.

The road may twist, and skies may darken,
Yet hope ignites a flame so bright.
With courage held, we keep on harkening,
To love and light that guide the night.

In silent battles, we find our way,
With every breath, a vow we make.
To face the dawn, to greet the day,
And tread the path, for our own sake.

So take my hand, let's walk as one,
Through unseen trails that lie ahead.
Together strong, we've just begun,
Resilience blooms where fears once bled.

Fleeting Shadows of Memory

In corners dim, the memories play,
Like whispers lost, they slip away.
A fragile thread, a gentle sigh,
Each moment fades, as time goes by.

Yet in the heart, they softly swell,
Those fleeting tales we know so well.
With laughter bright, and tears that glisten,
In quiet nights, our thoughts still listen.

Each photograph, a frozen dawn,
A snapshot of a life now gone.
In every smile, in every tear,
The echoes linger, ever near.

The shadows dance, the light does wane,
Yet in their grace, there's joy and pain.
We hold them close, these fragments clear,
In fleeting shadows, love draws near.

For though they fade, they never leave,
In every heart, they learn to weave.
A tapestry of what once was,
Fleeting shadows, love's warm cause.

Etched Beneath the Skin

In every scar, a story told,
Of battles fought, both brave and bold.
The skin a canvas, life's design,
With every mark, a tale divine.

The whispers of the past reside,
In quiet moments, seldom wide.
A laugh, a tear, they intertwine,
Etched beneath the skin, we shine.

Through trials faced, each wound a note,
A hymn of strength, in hearts we wrote.
In gentle touch, we find the light,
That guides us back, through darkest night.

In unity, our stories blend,
Like rivers flowing, never end.
We wear our lives, both flawed and real,
Etched beneath the skin we heal.

So let us honor every line,
Each mark a part of what is mine.
For in our scars, the beauty's seen,
Etched beneath the skin, we glean.

The Quiet Battle Within

In silence deep, a war is fought,
Where thoughts collide, and lessons taught.
A struggle veiled, yet ever clear,
The quiet battle, felt so near.

With shadows cast, and doubts that creep,
The heart decides, yet cannot sleep.
A whisper soft, a gentle plea,
To find the strength, to just be free.

Each day a choice, a step to take,
To face the fears, for courage's sake.
In quiet moments, we find our kin,
As we embrace the battle within.

Through echoes deep, a voice resounds,
That tells us hope in love abounds.
So hold on tight to dreams that soar,
The quiet battle leads to more.

For every heart that learns to fight,
Emerges stronger, shines so bright.
In unity, we stand and win,
The quiet battle, peace within.

Facades of Fortitude

In shadows cast by silent fears,
We wear our masks to hide the tears.
A brave facade, we stand upright,
Yet tremors quiver in the night.

Each heart a fortress, locked and tight,
Hiding scars of endless fight.
Behind each smile, a story sprawls,
Of battles fought within these walls.

We march along the well-trod path,
Dancing lightly to escape wrath.
But in the silence, whispers scream,
Our fortitude is not what it seems.

As dawn breaks through the heavy haze,
We find the strength to earn our praise.
In every crack, resilience gleams,
A testament to broken dreams.

So let the world see our disguise,
The beauty painted o'er our cries.
For in this fight, we rise above,
A tapestry of pain and love.

Cracks in the Armor

Beneath the steel, a fracture lies,
Where doubts and fears begin to rise.
A chink appears, the light shines through,
Revealing all that we once knew.

Our battles fought with sharpened swords,
Yet deep inside, we seek our words.
Vulnerabilities exposed in grace,
In the cracks, our fears we face.

A shield may glisten, bright and bold,
But underneath, the truth unfolds.
We wear our scars like badges true,
For every wound, life taught us too.

As warriors clad in roughened skin,
We find the strength to let love in.
For every crack that's shown anew,
Becomes a path for hope to brew.

So let your heart not hide in shame,
Each battle won, it earns a name.
With every flaw, we shape our story,
In cracks, we find our hidden glory.

Dreams of Battlefields

In dreams we wander through the fields,
Where whispered courage always yields.
The clash of swords, the sound of shields,
In sleepy minds, our fate reveals.

Beneath the stars, the warriors sleep,
While history's shadows softly creep.
Yet every night that truth will call,
In dreams, we rise before the fall.

We chase the echoes of a fight,
In heart and soul, the spark ignites.
Each vision bold, a path we tread,
With every breath, we conquer dread.

The tides of war, they ebb and flow,
Yet through the dark, we'll learn and grow.
For in our dreams, the strongest stand,
Together bound, we make a stand.

So when the dawn begins to break,
Remember dreams for courage's sake.
For in each heart a battlefield lies,
Awaken strong, let spirits rise.

Beneath the Surface: An Untold Tale

Beneath the water, secrets hide,
Where whispered truths can't be defied.
The currents swirl with tales of yore,
In silence kept, forevermore.

We delve beneath the tranquil flow,
Where shadows cast the tales we sow.
Untaught lessons linger still,
In hidden depths, we find our will.

The ripples dance on surfaces clear,
Yet underneath, there's darkest fear.
With every wave and fleeting breath,
Lies the dance of life and death.

So let us dive where few may chase,
To seek the depths of our own grace.
For in each mystery dwells a spark,
An untold tale, igniting dark.

Embrace the depths, face what we find,
For every story reshapes the mind.
Beneath the surface, hearts unveil,
And in our depths, we weave the tale.

Whispers of the Untold

In shadows deep, secrets lie,
Faint voices beckon, soft as sighs.
Stories woven in the night,
Unveil the dreams, embrace the light.

Echoes linger in the air,
Silent truths that none can share.
Lost in time, yet bold and clear,
Whispers echo, drawing near.

Through the silence, hearts can feel,
Mysteries that time can't steal.
In every breath there's something new,
The untold tales, the hidden view.

Elders nod, the wise can see,
What was hidden, set it free.
In the quiet, find your way,
To the voices that softly play.

Beneath the stars, a dance unfolds,
Of light and dark, of tales retold.
Embrace the whispers, hold them tight,
For in the silence shines the light.

Beneath the Facade

Beneath the smile, a tear can hide,
Layers masked, a heart inside.
In the laughter, shadows dwell,
Unseen battles, silent hell.

Caught in moments, lost in time,
Searching for reason, a hidden rhyme.
Beneath the surface, stories spin,
A fragile heart, a tale within.

The echoes of doubt, they softly creep,
Behind closed doors, where secrets seep.
A painted mask, a careful guise,
Yet truth resides behind the eyes.

In the stillness, find the grace,
Peel the layers, embrace the space.
For beneath it all, a spark resides,
A blazing spirit that never hides.

Ephemeral Marks

Fleeting moments, time's own art,
Each breath a brushstroke, a beating heart.
In gentle whispers, memories fade,
Unraveled dreams in shadows laid.

Moments captured, fragile and bright,
Like fireflies dancing in the night.
Time's embrace, a lover's hand,
Ephemeral marks scattered like sand.

In laughter shared, in tears unspooled,
Life's tapestry woven, forever ruled.
Each fleeting second, a chance to feel,
The fragile thread, the moments steal.

As seasons change, so do we,
In every shift, we come to be.
Ephemeral marks, a canvas wide,
In every heartbeat, dreams collide.

The Unwritten History of Healing

In quiet corners, healing waits,
Stories untold, behind the gates.
Every scar holds a silent tale,
An unseen voyage, a whispered trail.

With every tear, a seed is sown,
From brokenness, the spirit's grown.
In shadows deep, light starts to swell,
In the silence, the heart can tell.

Threads of hope, they intertwine,
With every step, the stars align.
An unwritten path, so soft, so real,
In the journey, we learn to heal.

Echoes of wounds, a graceful dance,
Through pain and love, we find our chance.
A history rich, yet never penned,
In the tapestry of life, we mend.

Unrecorded Heartbeats

In silence, whispers flow,
Unheard beats of dreams aglow.
Time slips gently, unconfined,
A symphony of love entwined.

Moments lost in fleeting haze,
Echoes dance through twilight's maze.
Hearts uncharted, paths unknown,
Each thump a tale of its own.

Fleeting glances pass us by,
Like stars that flicker in the sky.
In every sigh, a wish concealed,
In every pulse, a fate revealed.

Fragments drift on winds of chance,
As shadows weave a timeless dance.
With every breath, a story grows,
In beats of love, our essence glows.

Unrecorded, yet we know,
In each heartbeat, seeds will sow.
A tapestry of lives entwined,
In silent rhythms, we are aligned.

Sorrow in Shades of Gray

It lingers softly, like a sigh,
A muted ache that won't comply.
In shadows cast where feelings lay,
There lives a truth in shades of gray.

The echoes of a love once bright,
Now soften into fading light.
Every tear a story told,
In hues of sorrow, bright yet cold.

The whispers haunt in empty space,
Memories paint a somber face.
Each glimpse a ghost of what once was,
A heart now bound by hidden flaws.

We wander through the misty night,
Searching for the lost daylight.
Yet in the gray, there's beauty found,
In quiet grace, we still stand ground.

From sorrow's depths, we must arise,
To seek the dawn beyond the skies.
In shades of gray, we come to learn,
From every scar, our souls still burn.

The Unseen Navigator

Beneath the stars, a path unwinds,
A guide unseen, where fate reminds.
In dreams, we tread on destinies,
With whispered winds and rustling trees.

Through misty nights, the compass sways,
Charting journeys in secret ways.
Though shadows lurk and doubts arise,
The unseen hand ignites the skies.

In every twist, the heart explores,
Unlocking paths through hidden doors.
With every choice, a dance unfolds,
The navigator's touch it holds.

We wander on, lost yet aware,
In silence, trust the unseen care.
No map to guide, yet still we roam,
For in our hearts, we find our home.

Through storm and calm, we'll find our way,
With faith as light through night and day.
The unseen navigator's grace,
Will lead us to a warm embrace.

Radiance through the Shadows

In twilight's grip, a spark does glow,
A beacon bright, where shadows flow.
From darkness springs a gentle light,
Radiance that defeats the night.

Among the trees, a dance begins,
As soft whispers drown out the sins.
In every heartbeat, warmth ignites,
With hope reborn from wretched plights.

As stars align in cosmic streams,
We rise from ashes, chase our dreams.
Through hidden paths, we'll find the way,
Where radiance dispels the gray.

A journey long, yet not in vain,
For every loss, there's much to gain.
In shadows cast, the light we see,
A testament to what can be.

Embrace the dawn, release the past,
In every moment, love is cast.
Together we will stand and sing,
For radiance through shadows brings.

The Quiet Echo of Suffering

In shadows deep, whispers sigh,
A heart once bold, now wears a lie.
Silent cries and muted tears,
Reflect the weight of hidden fears.

Each breath a battle, each thought a chain,
Yet still we rise through phantom pain.
Beneath the scars, a flicker glows,
In hushed tones, true strength grows.

Ghosts of sorrow linger near,
Yet we learn to face our fear.
For pain's a canvas, rich and wide,
Where courage paints the soul's inside.

With echoes faint, we find our way,
Through the shadows and the gray.
In the quiet, hope takes flight,
Guided by the distant light.

Tattered Pages of the Past

In forgotten books, stories lie,
Pages worn, a time gone by.
Each tear a tale, each fray a fight,
Memories dance in the dimming light.

Whispers of joy, shadows of pain,
Ink of sorrow, sunlight and rain.
Binding fragile, yet deeply held,
Within these tales, our truths are spelled.

Lost directions, a winding road,
Heavy burdens, a silent load.
Yet from the ashes, new tales bloom,
In the remnants, love finds room.

Each tattered sheet a bridge to heal,
Lessons learned that time reveals.
In every chapter, whispers call,
And in our courage, we stand tall.

Veils of Resilience

Softly woven, threads of grace,
Frayed edges hide a fierce embrace.
Beneath the pain, a spirit stands,
In silent strength, we make our plans.

Through storms of doubt, we learn to fight,
Guided by the hope of light.
Each layer worn, a story told,
In bonds unbroken, hearts grow bold.

Veils of past, we honor still,
Yet forge ahead with iron will.
In every trial, a lesson found,
In every setback, strength unbound.

Resilient hearts, through fire, soar,
Finding peace forevermore.
In the dance of life, we sway,
Embracing night, welcoming day.

The Canvas of Hidden Hurt

Every stroke tells a story true,
Painted in shades of various hue.
On the canvas, tears become art,
Crafted beauty from a fractured heart.

In silence, chaos paints the night,
Yet through the darkness, we find light.
Brush of time, with gentle hand,
Transforms the pain, helps us stand.

Colors blend, creating depth,
Every line a lover's breath.
In every shadow, healing sigh,
A whisper of how we learn to fly.

Hidden hurt becomes our muse,
In heartfelt strokes, we learn to choose.
Our canvas wide, our spirits free,
Life's masterpiece, eternally.

The Invisible Cost of Courage

With each brave step, fear lingers close,
Silent whispers in the heart, morose.
A sunset painted with hues of dread,
For every triumph, a tear unshed.

Behind the smiles, battles remain,
A warrior's heart, bearing the pain.
In the shadows where doubt takes its toll,
Courage is forged by the quiet soul.

The cost is measured in sleepless nights,
In the aching hope for distant sights.
But every scar tells a tale of strength,
In the journey, we find our true length.

Faltering breaths may escape at times,
In the rhythm of life, a silent chime.
Yet the heart beats on, fierce and unbowed,
Courage awoken, fierce and proud.

So raise your voice against the unseen,
In the depths of the dark, let your light gleam.
For courage holds a price we must pay,
But it's the price that leads us to sway.

Traces of Love and Loss

In whispered dreams, our laughter plays,
Yet echoes linger in the freyed days.
Love, a ghost that softly calls,
In every shadow, the heart recalls.

The touch of hands now turned to air,
In every silence, I'm aware.
Memories dance in the fading light,
Tracing paths through the deep of night.

Moments shared, now bittersweet,
In every corner, love's pulse beats.
Yet loss remains, a heavy chain,
Binding the heart, delivering pain.

We carry the weight of what we had,
In every smile, a trace of sad.
Yet in the depths, a spark still glows,
For love eternal, through loss it flows.

So here I stand, amidst the ache,
In the field of memories, love won't break.
For even in loss, I find a trace,
Of love's embrace, a sacred space.

Underneath the Veil of Normalcy

Beneath the surface, secrets dwell,
In every smile, a hidden shell.
The world spins on, a masquerade,
Where truth and facade rarely fade.

In crowded rooms, we wear our masks,
Hiding the heart while the spirit tasks.
Conversations casual, yet so profound,
In the mundane, the lost are found.

Life's a tapestry, threads intertwined,
Each stitch a story, carefully lined.
Yet in the fabric, the silence hums,
As dreams echo softly, waiting, it comes.

Routine sways us to forget the fight,
But beneath the calm, there brews the night.
In the quiet corners, thoughts collide,
Where whispers of longing dare to abide.

So let us gaze beyond the plain,
To the hidden truths that still remain.
For underneath the veil of what we see,
Lies the essence of what's yet to be.

Shadows of Unvoiced Tomorrows

In the twilight of thoughts unshared,
Lies a world of dreams, unpaired.
Silent wishes in the fading light,
Casting shadows that blur the sight.

The weight of words held deep inside,
In the quiet moments, I confide.
Unsung hopes linger in the air,
Longing for voices that once were there.

Each tomorrow carries whispers sweet,
Yet echoes fade in the rushing feet.
Unvoiced dreams pulse beneath the skin,
Yearning to rise, to breathe again.

In shadows cast by unspoken fears,
A labyrinth of both hopes and tears.
Yet in the silence, a strength is found,
As the heart beats steady, profound.

So dare to dream beyond the night,
Let the shadows glean your light.
For in the silence of what's not said,
Lies the promise of all that's ahead.

Secrets Carved in Silence

Whispers linger in the night,
Shadows dance in muted light.
Every heart holds tales untold,
Carved in silence, brave and bold.

Behind the smiles, the pain resides,
In hidden corners, sorrow hides.
Yet through the quiet, hope can bloom,
In whispered dreams, dispelling gloom.

Secrets woven into the past,
In silent moments, shadows cast.
Each breath carries, a song unheard,
In the void, strength is stirred.

So hold the silence, let it speak,
In gentle quiet, the strong are meek.
What's left unsaid can still inspire,
A flicker of hope, a burning fire.

In silence, we find our peace,
A calming stillness that won't cease.
With every secret, a bond grows tight,
In the dark, we find our light.

Beneath the Mask of Composure

A smile hides the heart's true face,
Behind the mask, a silent grace.
Layered thoughts, like echoes blend,
Composure's veil we often tend.

Eyes may sparkle, laughter rings,
Yet silence hums of deeper things.
Beneath the surface, tides do sway,
In every word, a hidden way.

We wear our armor, brave and proud,
Yet carry burdens, lost in crowd.
Each gesture meant to mask the strain,
Within the calm, a world of pain.

But in the quiet, strength ignites,
With every breath, we claim our rights.
To show the world our true intent,
A heart that's strong, yet heaven-sent.

So peel the layers, let it flow,
Embrace the truth, let feelings show.
For beneath the mask, we find our core,
A deeper love, forevermore.

The Stories We Carry in Silence

Burdens held in quiet grace,
Stories etched on every face.
In gentle glances, tales unfold,
In whispered dreams, the brave and bold.

With every heartbeat, a tale to share,
Courage wrapped in tender care.
Silence, like a friend, will keep,
The secrets that we dare not weep.

In the shadows, truths collide,
Hopes and fears we try to hide.
Yet in the stillness, we can find,
Strength that ties the heart and mind.

The weight we bear, a shared refrain,
In silent moments, we know the pain.
Each story woven in the night,
Brings forth a quiet, guiding light.

So listen closely, hear the sound,
In silence, deeper truths are found.
The stories we carry, heavy yet bright,
Illuminate the path, leading to light.

The Depth of Hidden Strengths

In silence lies a hidden might,
A strength that blooms beyond the fight.
Veiled in shadows, yet so profound,
In heartbeats' rhythm, power is found.

Every struggle, each stumble back,
Builds the courage from what we lack.
In quiet moments, the soul takes flight,
Emerging gently into the light.

The whispers of fear may cross our mind,
Yet deeper currents help us bind.
With every breath, the truth we trace,
Strength like water finds its place.

So in the silence, hear the call,
The depth of strength is found in all.
Embrace the quiet, let it teach,
The truths that words may never reach.

From hidden depths, our spirits soar,
Unseen power forevermore.
In silence, we find our way to stand,
Stronger together, hand in hand.

The Depths of Hidden Lament

In shadows deep where sorrows creep,
A silent tear, a secret weep.
Wounds concealed where whispers play,
Memories haunt the light of day.

The heart bears weight, too much to share,
Behind a smile, a heavy glare.
Each thought a ghost, each breath a theft,
A silent scream, the echo left.

In stillness, aches are softly spun,
A dance of grief that's never done.
Connection lost in faded light,
A tale of pain, out of sight.

Yet in the dark, a flicker glows,
The strength to rise when no one knows.
Each tear, a thread in woven grief,
A tapestry of silent relief.

The world moves on, unmindful still,
Yet in our hearts, we bend, we will.
Through hidden strife, we find the way,
A buried truth in soft decay.

Threads of Concealed Heartache

Beneath the smiles, a shadow lies,
A heart entangled in quiet sighs.
In every laugh, a burden's trace,
Threads of pain time can't erase.

Silent nights and whispered dreams,
A delicate thread that slowly seams.
Between the joys, the heartache hides,
A secret dance the soul abides.

In crowded rooms, we're alone, yet close,
A tapestry where no one knows.
Echoes linger, slight and frail,
A heart's lament, a muted wail.

Yet each new dawn, we gather strength,
To weave our pain in measured length.
With every breath a hope unfolds,
For hidden hearts, their stories told.

In time we find that wounds can heal,
The secret joys that pain conceal.
Through threads of loss, we stitch a part,
A quilt of love in each brave heart.

A Tapestry of Secret Sorrows

In woven strands of muted hue,
A tapestry of sorrow grew.
Each thread a tale of heart betrayed,
In silence kept, in shadows laid.

The colors blend in quiet strife,
Moments lost in the fabric of life.
Behind closed doors, the echoes play,
Secret sorrows in disarray.

Yet in the weft, a strength remains,
Resilience pulls through all the pains.
With gentle hands, we mend and weave,
A hidden grace we dare believe.

Through tear-stained cloth, the stories shine,
Of love long lost, in thin design.
Each stitch a prayer, a whisper kind,
In secret sorrows, hope we find.

The loom of life, it carries on,
With every dawn, the light is drawn.
And through the fray, we come to see,
The art of living sets us free.

Chronicles of the Overlooked

In corners dim where shadows dwell,
The stories whispered, hard to tell.
Lives entwined in silent grief,
Chronicles lost, a fragile leaf.

Beneath the surface, pain abides,
In every heart, a secret hides.
Each glance a veil, a tale undone,
Moments passed, like rays of sun.

Yet in the quiet, strength will rise,
Voices echo, touching skies.
Through overlooked, we find our way,
A brighter sense in shades of gray.

We gather 'round, the stories blend,
A chorus loud, with hearts to mend.
For every tale, a thread connects,
Chronicles shared, the soul reflects.

In unity, our pains reveal,
The strength within that starts to heal.
Together we weave an endless thread,
In chronicles of lives well-led.

Whispers of Forgotten Wounds

In shadows deep, the silence creeps,
Old scars remember, yet seldom speak.
Time drips like rain, on barren ground,
Hidden stories in whispers found.

Each breath a chance, to mend the past,
Yet the echoes cling, they hold steadfast.
A heart that fractures, learns to heal,
But the whispers tell what we conceal.

Beneath the layers, the pain resides,
Between the laughter, where sorrow hides.
In the dark corners, the heart must wade,
Through echoes of love that never fade.

With every sunrise, hope flickers bright,
Yet shadows linger, veiling the light.
In the dance of healing, we find our way,
Through whispers of wounds, we dare to stay.

The Subtle Cost of Survival

In the hustle of life, we pay a fee,
A quiet toll, no one can see.
Moments of joy, often masked in pain,
Survival's cost has much to gain.

Every choice we make, a weight we bear,
Chasing dreams while wading through despair.
In every heartbeat, a sacrifice lied,
The subtle cost we often hide.

Friendships fray, as time slips away,
Beneath the surface, we often sway.
In the name of progress, we sometimes lose,
Valuable lessons, we refuse to choose.

Yet within the struggle, strength is born,
From the ashes, new paths are sworn.
The cost reminds us to seek and adapt,
Finding beauty in life's intricate map.

Beneath the Surface of Smiles

A smile can mask a tidal wave,
Beneath, the heart's a quiet grave.
With every laugh, a story fades,
Shadows linger in joyful charades.

We wear our masks, a colorful guise,
Hiding the truths that haunt our eyes.
In the lively chatter, silence grows,
Beneath the surface, the sadness flows.

Connections fray in the noise and cheer,
As we dance around what we truly fear.
Yet in the stillness, truth can emerge,
A gentle whisper, the heart's soft urge.

To seek the depths beneath the facade,
And find the strength to unmask the charade.
For in vulnerability, we find our strength,
In the depths of pain, we find love's length.

Hidden Layers of Grief

Grief wraps around, a cloak unseen,
Each layer thickens, as time creeps in.
Beneath the smiles, the heart does ache,
In subtle moments, we bend and break.

Memories linger like shadows cast,
Whispers of love in the echoes past.
Time may dull, but it cannot erase,
The hidden layers we cannot face.

In quiet nights, the tears may flow,
Releasing burdens, allowing the glow.
For grief is a journey, not a place,
In every step, we find our grace.

To cherish the joys, amidst the pain,
And honor the love that forever remains.
Through hidden layers, we learn to cope,
In the depths of sorrow, there lies our hope.

Fragmented Reflections

Shattered glass on the floor,
Memories whisper and soar.
Each piece tells a tale,
Of journeys set to sail.

Shadows dance in the light,
Echoes of those lost in night.
Reflections flicker with pain,
Mirrors of joy and disdain.

Stepping through the broken shards,
Finding beauty in the scars.
Fragments held in our hands,
Stories written in sands.

Colors blend, distort the truth,
Childhood dreams and lost youth.
In the chaos, we find grace,
Embracing the fractured space.

In silence, we start to mend,
Piecing together, till the end.
Each reflection brings a spark,
Lighting pathways from the dark.

Beneath the Armor

Beneath the surface, fears abide,
Hidden where the heart must hide.
Layers thick, a daunting wall,
   Yet inside, a tender call.

Courage shields what's felt inside,
But in the stillness, we collide.
Guarded hearts seek to be free,
   Longing for authenticity.

In whispered hopes, we dare to dream,
To let down walls, to find the seam.
Armor heavy, yet it breaks,
   Revealing all that love creates.

In moments shared, the mask won't stay,
Knowing bloom is born from fray.
Stripped of pretense, we can see,
   The beauty of vulnerability.

Trust unveiled beneath the light,
Unlocking secrets, day and night.
Together we can truly be,
   Beyond the armor, wild and free.

Veins of Untold Stories

In the quiet, stories flow,
In every heart, a tale we sow.
Veins filled with laughter and woes,
Hidden where the river flows.

Every crack holds a refrain,
Echoes of joy, whispers of pain.
In the silence, lives collide,
Breath of truth we often hide.

Navigating paths never shown,
In shadows, seeds of hope are sown.
Stories weave like threads of gold,
Binding hearts both young and old.

Footsteps mark the earth so wide,
With every stride, we redefine.
In every heartbeat, there we find,
The threads that link us, intertwined.

Listen close; their chorus sings,
Of love, of loss, of tiny wings.
Veins pulse with each untold flight,
In the tapestry of night.

The Space Between Heartbeats

In the stillness, moments pause,
Time can blur without a cause.
Between the beats, breath is found,
Silence speaks without a sound.

In the gap where dreams reside,
Hope blooms and fears abide.
In every tick, a choice we make,
In every pause, our chances shake.

The world spins in a gentle sway,
Yet in the quiet, we can stay.
Drifting softly through the air,
Finding solace, stripped bare.

What lingers in the empty space?
A memory, a warm embrace.
It's in these seconds we can see,
The beauty of simplicity.

Together, let's cherish the pause,
In the silence, life withdraws.
Heartbeats echo, and in between,
We find the moments yet unseen.

Secrets in the Silence

In whispers soft, the shadows play,
A world unseen, where echoes sway.
Behind closed doors, lost hopes entwine,
In secrets held, the heart may pine.

The quiet hum of thoughts unspun,
Where dreams reside, yet none are won.
In darkened corners, fears reside,
But in the hush, a truth will bide.

Beneath the stillness, stories crawl,
A tapestry of rise and fall.
In muted tones, reality bends,
While silence keeps, and sorrow mends.

With every breath, the weight we bear,
In quietude, the soul lays bare.
To listen close, the heart must dare,
For in the silence, love's laid bare.

Beneath the Bright Facade

A painted smile on troubled days,
A dance of light, a masked malaise.
The laughter hides a tear-stained truth,
Beneath the bright, the fading youth.

Behind the gloss, a heart that's bruised,
A vibrant life, yet deeply used.
In crowded rooms, the lonely ache,
While every glance is but a fake.

The shimmering skin, a fragile guise,
Conceals the storm within the skies.
In shadows cast by dazzling light,
Reality shimmers, out of sight.

Yet in the cracks, the beauty grows,
A richer story sweetly flows.
For even hearts that hurt can sing,
Beneath the bright, new blooms take wing.

The Canvas of Heartache

With each brushstroke, pain unfolds,
A vivid tale that time beholds.
In colors deep, the sorrow bursts,
On canvas wide, the heart it thirsts.

The hues of blue and shades of gray,
Compose the nights that steal the day.
In swirling lines, lost moments roam,
A masterpiece that feels like home.

Each layer tells of love's sweet woe,
Of whispered dreams we let go slow.
In every frame, the echoes creep,
The art we make, the tears we keep.

As shadows dance, the story's penned,
With strokes of loss, our hearts ascend.
Through heartache's veil, we learn to see,
The beauty born from agony.

Unraveled Threads of Time

In strands of gold, the past entwines,
With memories soft as olden lines.
Each thread a whisper, gently worn,
A tapestry of love reborn.

Moments stitched with joy and strife,
Woven patterns tell of life.
As time unwinds, the fibers fray,
Yet in the fraying, truths will stay.

Through years we drift, yet somehow thread,
In silent ties, the lost are led.
With hands of time, we weave and mend,
An endless cloth that knows no end.

Each knot a story, each tear a seam,
In life's grand quilt, we chase the dream.
Though threads unravel, the heart aligns,
In love's embrace, true light still shines.

Echoes of Silent Struggles

Whispers in the night, unheard,
Battles waged beneath the skin.
Courage hidden, dreams deferred,
Hope flickers where fear had been.

Voices lost in crowded rooms,
Tales of pain, wrapped tight in smiles.
Every heartbeat softly looms,
Bearing secrets, hidden trials.

Shadows linger, tightly pressed,
Tears unshed, a silent plea.
Finding solace in the rest,
Of unspoken harmony.

Yet the dawn will bring its light,
With every break of silent gloom.
Through the dark, we hold on tight,
To the promise of bloom.

Through the echoes, we have grown,
Weathered storms, we stand as one.
In the struggle, seeds are sown,
To rise anew with morning sun.

The Depths of Overlooked Sorrows

In the corners, shadows dwell,
Whispers lost in busy streets.
Unseen battles weave a spell,
In quiet hearts, the sorrow beats.

Tears that trickle, rarely shown,
Pain that lingers, hard to trace.
In the silence, truths are sown,
A heavy heart finds no embrace.

Forget-me-nots sprout from gloom,
Fading echoes from the past.
Grief and love in one small room,
Silent moments often last.

Yet in dawn, a light appears,
Hope, a fragile, gentle thread.
From the depths of hidden fears,
New beginnings may be bred.

Through the shadows, we shall rise,
Braving paths of thin and steep.
Every tear will re-energize,
In the promise of new leaps.

Tattered Pages of the Soul

Faded words on crinkled sheets,
Echoes of the life we've penned.
Stories lost in quiet streets,
Fragments haunt, as we pretend.

Scattered dreams of days gone by,
Worn-out tales of love and strife.
With each page, a silent cry,
Pages turning in this life.

Ink-touched memories collide,
Chapters written, lessons learned.
With each scar, the heart's been tried,
But through fire, hope's flame burned.

Every tear, a well-spun tale,
In the margins, truth will grow.
Through the storms, we will prevail,
Harvest strength from seeds we sow.

In the book of all we are,
Each tattered edge tells our fight.
With every line, we reach the stars,
Holding fast to our own light.

Imprints of Yesterday

Footprints left on sandy shores,
Whispers of the past we tread.
Moments lost, yet memory soars,
In echoes of what once was said.

Threads of time weave through the heart,
Stitching tales both bright and dim.
Past and present will not part,
In every laugh, in every hymn.

Lingering scents of sunlit days,
Remind us of a fleeting joy.
In twilight's glow, the heart still sways,
Whatever fate may seek to toy.

Through the lens of aching time,
We learn to walk both bold and slow.
In the journey, our hearts climb,
Embracing all that life may show.

Imprints left, a treasured guide,
Rooted deep in our souls' seam.
With every step, we turn the tide,
Creating space for what we dream.

Hidden Stories of the Heart

In whispers soft, the stories weave,
Between the beats, secrets we believe.
Each memory tucked, a fragile art,
In shadows deep, hidden stories start.

A glance, a touch, unspoken ties,
Through laughter's light and silent sighs.
They linger close, yet drift apart,
Echoes felt, the hidden heart.

In whispered dreams, we hold them tight,
A dance of souls in the quiet night.
Each tale a thread, a sacred part,
In the tapestry of the heart.

Sometimes they break, the fragile seams,
Yet in their cracks are whispered dreams.
A love that grows, though worlds may part,
Still burns within, the hidden heart.

The stories flow, a river's course,
Of joy, of pain, an endless source.
In quiet places, we chart the chart,
To find the truth of the hidden heart.

Invisible Wounds

Beneath the skin, the shadows lie,
A silent ache, a stifled cry.
No scars to see, yet pain runs deep,
Invisible wounds that never sleep.

With every smile, a mask we wear,
Yet in our eyes, the weight we bear.
Secrets held beneath the light,
Invisible battles, a quiet fight.

Every heartbeat tells a tale,
Of dreams that falter, of spirits frail.
In silent rooms, where whispers leak,
Invisible wounds, our hearts to speak.

As time goes on, we mend and break,
With every step, the choices we make.
Yet through the pain, we find the spark,
To rise again from the deepest dark.

For in our scars, a story's spun,
Of battles lost and victories won.
Invisible wounds, they shape our art,
In resilience found, we heal the heart.

Silent Battles Within

In quiet corners, battles rage,
A silent war, a binding cage.
Enemies born within ourselves,
In hushed tones, our secret dwells.

Each day a choice, a step or fall,
In darkened halls, we hear the call.
Voices clash, both wild and tame,
In silent battles, we play the game.

With every tear, a story spills,
Of dreams unchained and broken wills.
Yet hope persists, a gentle tide,
Through silent battles, we will abide.

In shadows cast, we learn to fight,
Turning pain into our light.
A journey long, yet we begin,
To find the peace so deep within.

For every struggle, a prize awaits,
Through silent battles, we unlock gates.
And in the end, we rise anew,
Fighting still, but stronger too.

The Weight of Unseen Thorns

Beneath the surface, thorns lie still,
A hidden weight, a restless will.
They pierce the heart, though eyes can't see,
The burden carried, just like me.

In crowded rooms, we wear our guise,
But in the silence, our truth defies.
Each thorn a mark on the soul's retreat,
The weight we bear, bittersweet.

Yet in the dark, we find the light,
Turning our pain into a flight.
With every step, we shed the weight,
Transforming thorns into our fate.

Through valleys deep and mountains tall,
We rise again from every fall.
The unseen thorns may hold us tight,
But in their clutch, we find our might.

For every thorn that pricks and tears,
A lesson learned, a heart that dares.
The weight we feel, in time won't bind,
For in our souls, true strength we find.

The Silent Constellation

In the night sky, they gleam so bright,
Whispers of dreams, calm and light.
Stars in silence, tales untold,
Silent constellations, ancient and bold.

Guiding hearts through shadows cast,
Glimmers of hope from the past.
Each twinkle a wish, a heartfelt tune,
In the vastness, beneath the moon.

Stories woven in cosmic threads,
Echoes of love where starlight spreads.
Their light a beacon, soft and true,
In the silence, they're here for you.

Infinite distances, yet we feel near,
In the calm darkness, there's little fear.
A tapestry of light, divine art,
Silent constellations, they touch the heart.

Ripples in the Stillness

Gentle waters reflect the sky,
In the stillness, moments lie.
Ripples dance in perfect grace,
Whispers echo in this space.

Calmlike silence, secrets kept,
In quiet depths, the world has slept.
Beneath the surface, life abounds,
In stillness, a symphony of sounds.

Nature breathes, a soft sigh,
Every ripple tells a why.
A canvas painted in hues serene,
Dreams interwoven in every sheen.

Time will linger, not rush past,
In the quiet, memories last.
Ripples in stillness, a soothing balm,
In this moment, the heart feels calm.

Tides of Hidden Grief

Beneath the surface, shadows flow,
Tides of sorrow, ebb and glow.
A heart weighed down by silent screams,
Lost in the depths of unspoken dreams.

Each wave carries a weight unseen,
Burdened souls in spaces between.
In the silence, pain resides,
As the ocean of feelings abides.

Memories wash ashore like sand,
Emotions tangled, hard to stand.
In flows of water, truth is found,
A tender ache that knows no sound.

With each tide, the heart learns to grieve,
Healing comes, if we believe.
Tides may rise, yet they recede,
From hidden grief, we gain our creed.

Voices Lost in the Crowd

In the bustling streets, voices collide,
Echoes of laughter, whispering pride.
Yet in the throng, one can feel small,
Voices get lost, barely a call.

Faces pass, a fleeting glance,
Every soul in its own dance.
Stories unshared, dreams held tight,
In the crowd's roar, fading from sight.

Searching for meaning in distant smiles,
Yearning for connection across the miles.
Among the throng, hearts beat alone,
In the silence, longing for home.

Yet in the chaos, light will break,
Voices rise with every awake.
Though lost now, they will be found,
In unity's song, a beautiful sound.

Shadows of Resilience

In twilight's grasp, we stand so tall,
Each shadow whispers, tales of all.
Through storms we've wandered, hearts so brave,
In silence, strength, our souls we save.

With every stumble, we rise again,
A dance of hope through endless pain.
Each tear we shed, a seed to sow,
In gardens bright, our spirits grow.

The weight of trials, a bridge to cross,
In unity, we count the loss.
Together forged, in flames we shine,
Resilience blooms in life's design.

Faint echoes call from deep within,
A symphony where we begin.
With every heartbeat, know it's real,
In shadows' depth, our light will heal.

The night may cloak our fragile dreams,
Yet inner strength, it softly gleams.
A tapestry of scars we weave,
In shadows' grace, we will believe.

Fragments of Broken Glass

Scattered pieces on the ground,
Silent stories, lost, yet found.
In jagged edges, beauty lies,
Reflections of our weary cries.

Each shard a moment, bright and dark,
A fleeting spark, a quiet mark.
Together forming, an artful tale,
In brokenness, we will prevail.

The light that bends through cracks we see,
A rainbow formed from what could be.
From shatters deep, resilience shows,
In every cut, a strength that grows.

We navigate through shards of pain,
In mosaic made of hurt and gain.
With gentle hands, we build anew,
From fragments lost, we find our view.

In chaos sings the heart's refrain,
An anthem born from joy and pain.
Together let us forge ahead,
From broken glass, our spirit's spread.

The Quiet Cost of Survival

In whispers soft, the price is paid,
Each breath a note, a debt we made.
In shadows cast, away we tread,
The cost of life, in silence spread.

Through sleepless nights, the battles rage,
Each heart a prisoner in a cage.
With weary hands, we grasp the grace,
Of moments fleeting, in time's embrace.

The choices weigh, the paths unfold,
In echoes harsh, the truth retold.
Yet still we strive, through broken dreams,
To find the light in distant beams.

We navigate through endless doubt,
With every step, we seek the route.
Though heavy hangs the quiet cost,
In life's vast sea, we'll not be lost.

For in our souls, a fire burns bright,
A guiding star through darkest night.
The quiet cost, a price we pay,
For in our hearts, hope finds its way.

Songs of the Undiscussed

In hushed tones, the stories breathe,
A melody we all believe.
In silence deep, the truths reside,
Behind closed doors, where fears abide.

Yet wisdom hums through whispered lines,
Each note a spark, our soul defines.
With unspoken words, we weave our song,
In unity where we belong.

The echoes fade, yet still we hear,
The voices wrapped in tender fear.
They rise like smoke, to fill the air,
A chorus born from hearts laid bare.

A tapestry of silent cries,
In shadows' arms, our spirit flies.
In unity, we share the fight,
With songs of hope, we claim the light.

So let us sing what's not discussed,
In hearts ablaze, in dreams we trust.
For every voice, a story's thread,
In harmony, our spirits spread.

Milton Keynes UK
Ingram Content Group UK Ltd.
UKHW021859151124
451262UK00014B/1331